T0169813

When You're Not OK

Jill Stark is an award-winning journalist and author with a career spanning two decades in both the UK and Australian media. She spent ten years on staff at *The Age* covering health and social affairs as a senior writer and columnist, and now works as a freelance journalist, media consultant, and speechwriter. Her first book, *High Sobriety*, was longlisted for the Walkley Book Award and shortlisted in the Kibble Literary Awards. Her second book, *Happy Never After*, is a self-help memoir about mental health.

When You're Not OK

a toolkit for tough times

Jill Stark

with illustrations by Carla McRae

SCRIBE

Melbourne • London

Scribe Publications
18–20 Edward St, Brunswick, Victoria 3056, Australia
2 John Street, Clerkenwell, London, WC1N 2ES, United Kingdom
3754 Pleasant Ave, Suite 100, Minneapolis, Minnesota 55409, USA

First published by Scribe 2019
This edition published 2020

Copyright © Jill Stark 2019
Illustrations copyright © Carla McRae 2019

All rights reserved. Without limiting the rights under copyright
reserved above, no part of this publication may be reproduced, stored in,
or introduced into a retrieval system, or transmitted, in any form or by
any means (electronic, mechanical, photocopying, recording or otherwise)
without the prior written permission of the publishers of this book.

The moral right of the author has been asserted.

Typeset in Portrait by the publishers

Printed and bound in Singapore by 1010 Printing Co Ltd

Scribe Publications is committed to the sustainable use of natural resources
and the use of paper products made responsibly from those resources.

9781950354115 (US edition)
9781925849332 (Australian edition)
9781912854622 (UK edition)
9781925693959 (e-book)

Catalogue records for this book are available from the
National Library of Australia and the British Library.

scribepublications.com

To all the warriors doing it tough — you are not alone

Contents

Author's Note

We all struggle. Some people might tell you that they don't, but they do. So let's start by acknowledging that you're normal. Not a single person on this planet can escape tough times. And if you secretly worry that you're weird or broken or unfixable, congratulations, that's normal, too.

Despite what social media's airbrushed amphitheatre might have us believe, sadness, anxiety, hurt, jealousy, loneliness, anger, disappointment, and the countless other forms of emotional turmoil we all experience are completely natural facts of life. They're what make us human.

But just because the struggle is real doesn't make it easy. There are days when hiding under the covers and blocking out the world seems like the safest bet. Sometimes the road gets so bumpy, it feels as if we'll never regain our footing. And when the ground beneath us is crumbling, it can be hard to navigate a way forward.

It's in those times that we need to take care of ourselves. But it's also usually in those times that we're at our most self-critical. I know how exhausting it can be to grapple with an internal saboteur perpetually saying, 'You're a bit shit.' My own saboteur is a master at magnifying shortcomings and obscuring any wins or strengths from view.

When things are bad, our internal critic can be deafening. And in an 'always on' digital age, where life's speed bumps and pitfalls are often filtered out of the picture, it can feel as if we're the only one drowning while everyone else is #blessed and living their bliss as they glide gracefully through their perfect lives.

Those are the days — or weeks or months — when we need reminding that we're not alone. It's in these times that we need to know that we're worth fighting for: that we can survive, that these feelings are not permanent, and that we will once again reach solid ground.

That's what this book offers — signposts to help you find the path back to yourself and advice on how to be OK, even when you're not. It's a guide for those moments when you just need a little help, an emotional first-aid kit to be cracked open when shit gets a little too real. Whether you're having a bad day, or a run of bad days that seems never-ending, these pages are filled with practical self-care tips for your body, mind, and soul.

It's also a book about learning to give yourself a break when things seem broken. This is *not* a book that's going to tell you to 'just stay positive' or suggest you grit your teeth, slap on a grin, and repeat 'I am strong, I am happy' affirmations in the mirror until your brain believes it. There's a special place in hell for purveyors of trite self-help bullshit and 'wellness inspo' that flies in the face of reality and preys on our insecurities. You won't get that from me.

What I will share with you are things I've found helpful when times are tough and my anxiety is peaking. Because I've been there before. In fact, I've been there so many times, I started thinking, 'I could write a book about this.' So I did. I should stress that I'm not a doctor or a psychologist. I'm not a counsellor, a spiritual guru, or a life coach. This book is not meant to be a prescriptive guide, nor should it act as a replacement for professional therapy or medical treatment. But I am someone who knows what it's like to be in a place where you have to fight your way through every moment. And I'm also someone with a brain that regularly lies to me.

I've struggled with chronic anxiety and periods of depression since I was a child. Even in the good times, my brain can be an unwieldy beast to manage. It likes to conjure up the most elaborately catastrophic predictions on everything from my health ('Oh my god, is this pimple actually a melanoma?') to my career prospects ('This is, without question, the worst thing you've ever written, everyone is going to see how much of a fraud you really are and demand your editor fire you from a cannon directly into the sun, where you will burn for all eternity just as you deserve').

It also offers me wildly unhelpful life advice such as '3.00 am is the best time to email your boss with detailed thoughts on their management style' or 'The reason your best friend hasn't returned your text message is because they either hate you or have died and you should definitely spend all day obsessing about which one it is until you are either drafting a lengthy apology or making funeral plans.'

Then there are the times where my brain just collapses in on itself. In 2014–15, I experienced a pretty serious breakdown that I nearly didn't survive. It was a long, hard road back to myself and I documented that journey in my memoir *Happy Never After: why the happiness fairytale is driving us mad (and how I flipped the script)*, which of course I highly recommend you check out!

The lessons I learned along the way — and continue to learn every day — about how to cope with the toughest times were explored at length in that book and have now been distilled into a more compact form in *When You're Not OK*, in a way that I hope is accessible, practical, and ultimately hopeful. This is the book to keep by the side of your bed or tuck into your bag for those days when you need a helping hand.

I know there is no one-size-fits-all approach to good mental health, nor is there a quick fix or secret formula. We are all unique and complicated and what works for me might not be 100 per cent right for you. But my hope is that there is something in here for everyone and you will find words that resonate with you and the way you experience the world.

I've divided these tips into self-explanatory sections to suit different moods and circumstances. Some of these tips contradict others in the book, because you need different advice for different situations. You can read it from start to finish or dip in and out, depending on what you need in that moment.

Oh, and one final thing — I'm not an 'influencer', so nothing I've written is sponsored content. When I recommend a book or an app, it's because I genuinely like it and found it helpful, not because I'm being paid to say so.

This is a book that won't encourage you to ignore your reality, nor will it patronise you with platitudes. But I hope it will help you navigate a gentler path through the tough times and make it easier to accept and embrace the wonderfully messy, complex parts of yourself that make you human.

Jill Stark
xo

1

Acceptance

I've read a *lot* of self-help books. When you're in a tough place, you look for answers wherever you can find them. But holy crap, there is some mind-blowingly bad advice out there. I've read far too many books filled with suggestions that make no sense or simply fly in the face of reality.

A recurring theme is that if you're feeling unhappy or anxious, you should do everything in your power to pretend you're not. One book gives this advice: 'Force yourself to smile in front of a mirror at least twice a day. As your face changes so your heart changes until the smile reaches your eyes and you feel warm inside.' Another suggested practising daily positive affirmations such as 'I shine with happiness' or 'I enjoy every moment of my life'.

This is the kind of life advice that I instinctively want

to hurl into the nearest fire. The positive-thinking movement is bullshit. Sure, it's important to try to look for the chink of light on the dark days, but that's not the same as grinning your way through a crisis or chuckling your way out of a panic attack. The fastest track to insanity is trying to convince yourself everything is OK when really it's not.

So let's stop doing that. You don't have to deny your feelings or 'fake it till you make it'. Let yourself feel whatever you're feeling. Believe me, the more you try to push away your discomfort, the more uncomfortable you'll be. It may feel counterintuitive at first, but if you ditch the affirmations and lean into the chaos, you'll be surprised how things can shift.

Cry loud and cry often

Sometimes you just have to cry until all the crying's done. Don't fight it. Ugly cry like you did when you were a little kid. Let the snot flow and the spit dribble from your bottom lip. Thump your fists on the ground, stamp your feet, and howl into the abyss.

You might want to designate a position and a place most suited to letting it all out. Face down on my hallway floor is where I do my best crying. I call it carpet grieving.

When you cry, it releases stress hormones. Tears are the body's way of letting out emotional pain. You'll often feel calmer after a good sob.

Accept love

Without question. Life is too short
to doubt human kindness, rebuff love,
or be timid with our emotions. Don't
hold back on telling the people you
love how much you care.

Emotional baggage

We all have it. Anyone who says they don't hasn't lived. Or they're not being honest. The trick is to learn how to carry that baggage with grace and purpose. Embrace your weird self. Be curious about your foibles. Remember that every single one of us is flawed and trying to figure our shit out. It's part of being alive.

Acceptance

Don't resist

The more you resist those painful, icky feelings, the longer they'll hang around. Pushing away pain only entrenches suffering. Make space for it. Recognise that it has a purpose. Anxiety is often a signal that something in our life is out of balance.

Opening up to the discomfort, rather than wishing it wasn't happening, can help you see what needs to change. As the thirteenth-century Persian poet Rumi said, 'The wound is where the light enters you.'

It's OK to bail

Sometimes a shit party is just a shit party.
Accept that you're not going to have the
time of your life every time you go out.
That doesn't make you strange or antisocial
or a Debbie Downer.

Remember that drinking more wine does
not magically make dull people more
interesting. Sometimes the best decision is
to head for the exit. That's totally fine.

Acceptance

Same old story

We all have stories we tell ourselves about who we are and why we do things. If you're like me, they're usually terribly unkind, wildly inaccurate distortions of reality that repeat on a loop, particularly in tough times. But they're just stories. A tired old narrative with the same hackneyed characters and plotlines.

List these themes in bullet points in a journal or on your phone and notice when you're reverting to the fictional story. Invariably, every word of self-critical trash talk will fit into one of a handful of recurring tropes.

Mine include: 'I am defective', 'I am helpless', 'I will never get better', and 'I am the problem child'. Observing the pattern helps me detach from the destructive force of the words and accept them for what they are — meaningless lines in a rehashed story.

Live outside
the box

You may have been diagnosed with
clinical depression or an anxiety disorder
or perhaps you just self-identify as 'damaged'
or a 'crazy person'. Even if those things are
true, don't let words box you in or define
you. Your mental state is something that
is happening *to* you. It is not who you are.
You are more than a label.

Shitty days

Accept them. They're not a character flaw or a sign you're going backwards. You're having a bad day, not a bad life. Don't attach a significance to the shitty days that they don't merit.

Acceptance

Make the broken beautiful

Just because you feel broken doesn't mean you are. In Japan, *kintsugi* is the ancient art of restoring broken pottery with fine powdered gold. When the cracks are painstakingly filled with luminous golden seams, it shows that nothing is ever beyond repair. The imperfections become part of a masterpiece.

We are constantly falling apart and putting ourselves back together. We might not look the same after we break, but we can still shine. Don't hide your scars. Wear them with pride. They are the gold that holds the vase together.

Happy
never after

It's not the default human position to be
happy all the time. Experiencing sadness,
grief, frustration, anger, loss, and the myriad
other emotions that life routinely throws
up is not something we can avoid.

And there's nothing wrong with you if you're
not blissfully happy 24/7. Strive for wholeness,
not happiness. That means accepting all
the feelings, even the tough ones.

Remember ...

We are all weird in our own way.
How wonderful is that.

2

The Basics

I've gone through periods in my life where getting out of bed was an enormous struggle — times when the simple act of existing was a chore, and all I could do was remind myself to breathe in and out and to keep putting one foot in front of the other until it was no longer a conscious effort.

It was during these tough times that I learned that, even on the darkest day, there were choices I could make to help me get through.

Sometimes, you just have to strip it right back to basics and take a moment-by-moment approach until the storm passes.

These are some small actions that on the good days you may take for granted, but on the hardest days can make a big difference.

Morning dread

When the road is rocky for me, mornings are always the worst. But I have to keep reminding myself that some of what I'm feeling is physiological. When we wake up, our bodies produce cortisol to give us energy and remind us it's time to get up. But it's the same hormone released when we're stressed, so it can be anxiety-inducing if you're already feeling on edge.

Try not to attach to the sensations in your body. Just let them be there and know they can't hurt you. Don't lie there ruminating on the feelings. Get out of bed, even if it's only as far as the couch. Try to get up. It will help.

Make your bed

I know, I know, some days you really don't
have the energy. But finding the strength
to pull up the covers and tuck in a sheet is
worth it. If nothing else, it's a clear demarcation
between day and night, helping to create
routine and making it less tempting to
fall back into bed.

Shower

Try not to go more than two days
without a shower. Even if you can't
face leaving the house, a hot shower
and the feeling of being clean is an
achievement in itself.

Change
your clothes

Some days, the kindest thing you can do
for yourself is stay in your pyjamas, make
a pillow fort on the couch, and binge watch
your favourite trash-fire TV show. But be
mindful of not letting your PJs become
your uniform.

Try to get dressed most days, even if you're
not going outside. Lay your clothes out
the night before if morning decisions
are a challenge.

Move your body

Have you left the house today? Change
your surroundings. It doesn't have to be a
ten-kilometre run or a hike through the
hills. A walk around the block will do.

Moving your body can help slow down
a chattering brain and make it easier
to sleep at night.

Put on your shoes and get outside. The first
few steps are always the hardest. If you're
not feeling it after ten minutes, give yourself
permission to come back. Nine times out
of ten, if you make it to ten minutes,
you'll keep going.

Change
your sheets

There's something comforting about
sliding into freshly laundered sheets. Even
if it takes you two hours and you're fighting
through tears at the sheer bloody effort of it
all and you have to take regular reality-TV
rest breaks and pour yourself a tea and lie on
the floor and bang your fists at the injustice
of not having a butler to do this shit for you,
it's an investment in yourself that always
feels so good once it's done.

Eat something — anything

Appetite can be one of the first things to go when you're stressed, depressed, or anxious. But you need energy to get through this. Try to put food in your body three times a day.

This is the point where I should say there's clear evidence that a nutritious diet benefits your mental health, but frankly, when you're struggling to keep your head above water, just eat whatever you can manage.

If that means ice cream and cake for breakfast and ordering in cheeseburgers

every night, then you do you. Obviously
it would be ideal if you ate lots of fresh
fruit and veggies, but you can focus on
a more balanced diet when your appetite
returns and eating is no longer a chore.
The most important thing for now
is to eat something.

Plan
your meals

The neon glare of a supermarket's strip
lights is no place to be making decisions.
At one low point, I had a total meltdown
in the canned-goods aisle trying to choose
between 64 varieties of tuna.

Before leaving the house, make a list of the
specific food products you need/can stomach.
If decisions are too hard, enlist a trusted
friend as your helper monkey.

And when you're in a better headspace,
you might want to bulk prepare meals you
can chuck in the freezer for times when
you can't face cooking or shopping.

Clean up

Resist the temptation to let the dishes
pile up in the sink. It's a lot less daunting
to clean one plate after you use it than it
is to scrub four-day-old congealed food
scraps off a stack of pots and pans and
bowls cluttering every surface.

When I'm anxious, I sometimes find
a cleaning frenzy helps release some of
that nervous energy and makes my
environment feel calmer.

Remember ...

If you're going through hell,
keep going.

3

<u>Love Your Body</u>

Taking care of your physical health when your emotional health is spiralling isn't always easy, but being kind to your body will help with your mood. And you don't have to make drastic life changes to see the benefits.

Here are some reminders of the physical things that can help and the ones that can harm when we're not feeling our best.

Exercise shouldn't suck

There is strong evidence that regular exercise can help alleviate the symptoms of anxiety and depression and be a preventative tool for managing stress. But it doesn't have to be a chore.

If you find the idea of running on a treadmill or lifting weights at the gym horrifying, don't do it. Exercise shouldn't be a punishment. Cycle or walk or swim or do yoga or join a salsa-dancing troupe or a roller-derby team. Find a way to move your body that you enjoy.

Stretch

Look, I'm a pretty basic yogi, so I'm not going to suggest you break out the upside-down scorpion or the wounded peacock, but some simple stretches combined with controlled, deep breathing for three to five minutes can help release body tension and slow down a racing mind. These are some of my fave anxiety busters:

Extended child's pose

Good for the knots in your back, neck, and shoulders. Kneel with your feet together, knees hip-width apart, and forehead touching the floor, and stretch your arms out on the floor in front of you as far as you can reach. Stretch forward a little further with each inhale, and then release all tension with the exhale.

Standing forward bend

Breathe in and raise your arms above your head, then fold your body forward from the hips, flopping like a rag doll to reach towards your toes, letting your shoulders, arms, and back become dead weights. I like to let everything go with my exhale as I drop, releasing a heavy 'uggghhh' noise as if I've just read a particularly egregious late-night tweet from Donald Trump.

Legs up the wall

So simple, but so effective in slowing the heart rate. Lie on your back next to a wall, shuffle your bum as close to the wall as possible, then raise your legs up the wall so their backs rest against it and your body is in an L-shape. With your arms resting on the floor by your side, palms up, take long deep breaths in and out.

Avoid caffeine

My brain's default position is to race at a
million miles an hour. It doesn't need any
chemical assistance. Caffeine is a stimulant,
making it the natural enemy to calm. Cut
back or cut out coffee, tea, and caffeinated
soft drinks if you're trying to slow down
a strung-out mind.

Stay hydrated

Being stressed makes me so thirsty.
All that over-breathing and tiredness
that comes with heightened anxiety can
cause a dry mouth and a general feeling
of dehydration. Make sure you drink lots
of water throughout the day. But don't
beat yourself up if you aren't storing water
like a thirsty camel. Two litres a day is
a great goal, but so is just having
a drink when you can.

Lay off the drugs

Zero judgement from me if you like
taking party drugs at the weekend, but
be wary of the comedown if you're having
a rough patch. For me, Saturday night's
serotonin high was followed by a crash that
I came to know as 'Suicide Tuesday'.
And that's why I haven't dabbled since
I was 22. Know your limitations and try
to stick to them.

High sobriety

That last glass of wine at 3.00 am is rarely a good idea. Alcohol is a natural depressant. It might feel like a few drinks 'take the edge off', but the next morning those edges are sharper and cut you deeper.

If you're not feeling OK, try to avoid using booze as a crutch. Drink moderately. Or if, like me, you're the kind of person who finds that a couple of beers can easily lead to a lost weekend, consider not drinking at all while you're in a tough place.

Beware hangxiety

If you do end up drinking more than you'd like, take it easy on yourself, and remember that hangovers make everything feel worse. That antsy, restless, 'the world's coming to an end' feeling you get, where you're drowning in a perfect storm of shame, nausea, and guilt, and questioning every decision you've ever made since the day you were born — that's hangxiety.

Don't make any major decisions in this state. Hangovers flood your body with adrenaline and cortisol, heightening anxiety and making it harder to relax. Accept that your nervous system is depleted, your

blood sugars are low, and your sleep has
been disrupted. Be kind to yourself and
know that this will pass.

Dance

Like no one's watching. Whenever you can.
Wherever you can. It's good for the body,
but more importantly, it's good for the soul.
Dance the way you did when you were a kid.
Cut loose. Let your body move whichever
way feels comfortable. Just dance.

Create a sleep routine

Stress is so tiring. It can make you sleep for 18 hours a day or make your mind so busy you're awake half the night. Getting into a routine can help regulate sleep and remind your brain when it's time to switch off. Try to go to bed at the same time every night and get up at the same time each morning.

Resist the urge to lie in bed all day. The less energy you expend, the more awake your body and mind will be at bedtime. When things are rough for me, I give myself a gold star every time I get up before 9.00 am.

Practise sleep hygiene

To maximise your chances of falling asleep, avoid caffeine, alcohol, or sugar at night.

Also, try to minimise time on your phone. The blue light from devices wreaks havoc with the body's natural circadian rhythms, so try not to look at phones, tablets, or laptops an hour before bed.

You want your bedroom to be as calm as possible, so if you're struggling to sleep and checking the time on your phone is causing more anxiety, consider leaving it in another room.

Remember ...

Rest is not an indulgence.
Listen to what your body needs.

4

Slow Down

Modern life is exhausting. We're over-scheduled, over-stimulated, and often tearing through the world at breakneck speed. The frantic pace of twenty-first-century living can exacerbate anxiety and make it feel as though we're trapped in a hamster wheel, furiously spinning and spinning, but going nowhere.

Finding calm means learning to live more slowly. It takes conscious effort to break out of the spin cycle, but it can be done. With some small adjustments, you can slow down your body and mind.

Meditate

Some days, sitting quietly with my own thoughts is like trying to restrain a dozen feral cats inside a string bag, so if you're turned off by the idea of meditation, I hear you.

But you don't need to empty your mind or reach a trance-like state of tranquillity. If you have a brain, you can meditate. It can be as basic as quietly focusing on your breathing for five minutes or lying on your back and repeating a simple mantra in your head.

Guided meditations are a helpful place to start. I use the app Calm, which has a range of really gentle practices from just two minutes all the way to half an hour. Even on the very worst days, I always feel a bit better when I'm finished.

Breathe

Slowly and deeply. In through your nose and out through your mouth. Five times. Repeat.

Be mindful

Spending a day hunched over a mindfulness colouring book or staring at the intricate grooves of a raisin for hours on end isn't going to solve all your problems, but practising being still and observant can help slow down a racing mind. It could be paying careful attention to the warm water as it hits your skin in the shower, noticing the different shapes and textures of the clouds overhead, or feeling your feet connect with the footpath as you walk.

For me, it's watching my cat, Hamish, sleeping. I take in every detail — the rusted tip of his nose, the signature tabby V-shape on his forehead, the gentle way his little pot

belly rises and falls as he snoozes.
It's a quick way to pause and ground
me in the moment.

Be in nature

Kick off your shoes. Let your bare feet touch the grass. Spending time in the natural environment has been shown to have a calming effect on the brain.

The Vitamin D you get from sunlight also helps improve mood, so leave your phone at home and visit your local park, beach, or bushland.

Pay attention to the sights, smells, and sounds. Listen to the wind rustling through the trees. Breathe in the salty air of the ocean. Slow down and watch the wildlife. Stay still and just observe.

The 'crazy busy' trap

Racing towards burnout shouldn't be a competitive sport. Don't wear 'crazy busy' as a badge of honour. If you're over-scheduled and pushing yourself to extremes in your personal or professional life, it's worth asking, What's driving that need to please?

What validation are you seeking from rushing around between one commitment and another? What void are you trying to fill? Stop trying to prove you're indispensable and give yourself permission to say *no*. It's OK to do less. Your value is not based on the content of your calendar.

Be like a cat

On one particularly bad day when everything seemed catastrophic and I couldn't stop crying, I noticed Hamish basking in the sun as it streamed through the lounge room window, and thought to myself, 'That looks so nice.'

So I got down on the rug and curled up next to him. The sunlight bathed my skin in warmth, and, for a moment, everything was OK. Be like Hamish. Bathe in a sun patch. Take an afternoon nap under a blanket on the couch. Stretch out your limbs, and just be still.

Find quiet

Actively seek it out. Don't put on your headphones every time there's a moment of silence. Listen to the sounds around you. Tune in to your environment. Let your thoughts breathe.

Muscle relaxation

My muscles ache when I'm in a super-anxious state, and often I don't even realise I'm tensed up until I become so knotted that my whole body stiffens. When I can afford it, I book in for a deep-tissue massage, but when that's not an option, I loosen the tension by practising progressive muscle relaxation. It also can help calm the body and mind down enough to drift off to sleep.

There are plenty of free apps you can download to guide you through a meditation that scans the whole body, tensing and releasing muscle groups to create a state of deep relaxation.

Do nothing

You don't have to be always 'doing'.
When was the last time you did absolutely
nothing? Not looking at your phone, reading
a book, watching TV, working on your
computer — just being? Spend some time
sitting still. Allow yourself to be bored.
Without downtime, there can be no creativity
or inspiration. Stare out the window.
Daydream. It's OK to press pause.

Remember ...

When you rush, you miss what's
right in front of you.

5

It Takes a Village

When you're not OK, it's normal to feel alone. The worries and stresses you're carrying can seem weird and unusual and completely unique to you. It's often a bewildering and lonely experience. But the more you internalise those 'crazy' thoughts and feelings, the more isolated you'll feel.

Don't suffer in silence. Talk to the people around you. Build a village of helpers — whether that's friends, family, colleagues, medical professionals, or just helpful books or blogs. Seek guidance and a soft place to fall wherever you can get it.

Support is critical when times are tough. Learning where to get it, how to ask for it, and who is a safe bet to offer it takes courage and practice. But sometimes you have to take the leap before the safety net can appear.

How does it feel?

Anxiety or emotional pain is different for everyone. And unlike a physical wound, it's not visible to the naked eye. It can be hard for loved ones to understand what's going on when they don't live inside your head. In calmer times, try to explain how your pain manifests itself, so that when you're in a moment of high stress, they have some idea what you're going through.

One of the analogies I use with friends is the sodden sponge. My brain can feel so waterlogged with catastrophic thoughts that I want to wring it out like a wet sponge. Other times, my mind is like an elastic band stretched to its tautest point, ready to snap. Find an analogy or description that helps people understand your stress.

Ask for what you need

People will try to help in ways that make sense to them, but which might not be best for you. Teach them how to support you. If you need a hug, ask for it. If you need to talk or would prefer company without words, say so. Sometimes you will need time alone to cry or reflect or heal or connect to yourself. Other times, the healthiest thing for you in that moment will be to be around people.

Perhaps you need help deciding what to eat or preparing food, or need someone to walk with you. Ask for what you need, and if you're not sure what that is, tell them that, too.

It might also help to ask the people close to you to keep you accountable. Tell them what

your goals are — it might be getting out of
the house every day or booking in with your
psychologist — and get them to check in
regularly to see how you're travelling.

Choose the right helper

No one person can fulfil all your needs. Different people in your life play different roles. Some friends will be the people you can collapse on, sobbing and bereft, in a crisis. Others will be better suited to making you laugh as a distraction from the pain. Choose the right person for the right role.

And remember, advice is often offered through the lens of someone's own experience. You can be grateful for suggestions, but you're not obliged to follow them.

Let them go

Life's too short to be surrounded by people who make you feel like a lesser version of yourself. If a friendship or relationship has turned toxic, or someone is draining all your energy, let them go.

Before you diagnose yourself with depression, make sure you're not just surrounded by dickheads. There will of course be times when your mood might make loved ones seem irritating or difficult when they're actually just trying to help, so make allowances for that when you're not at your best. But if someone consistently leaves you feeling depleted rather than nourished, it might be time

to reconsider the relationship. The same
goes for people you're hate-following on
social media. If they make your teeth
itch, cut them loose.

Pat a pet

A cat or a dog or a guinea pig, or any animal that enjoys human affection. Stroking a pet, or even just being in its company, has been shown to alleviate stress and lower blood pressure.

If you don't have your own, then maybe visit your local cat cafe or dog park. There are few things more life-affirming than watching a blissed-out pooch frolic off the leash.

Reach out

Sometimes it's just a bad day or a rough patch you can manage on your own. Other times, you need a bit more help. If you feel like you need support that friends and family can't provide, it might be time to book in with a doctor, psychologist, or counsellor.

I'm not going to pretend getting the right support is easy — I know first-hand the limitations of our mental-health system — but don't lose hope if your first attempt doesn't feel like the right fit. It can be a process of trial and error before you find a clinician you feel comfortable with, but it's worth persevering. Referrals from friends are a good place to start.

Medication

There is no magic pill for our emotional pain, but drugs may be a helpful part of the mental-health toolkit for some people in some circumstances. Talk to your GP or psychiatrist about options.

Everyone is different, but there is absolutely no shame in taking medication. If you're already on prescription drugs, don't change the dosage or stop taking them without the support of a medical doctor.

Whatever works

Everyone's an armchair expert when it comes to what you should and shouldn't do to look after your mental health, but don't let other people's judgement prevent you from trying alternative therapies that might help. I've tried reiki, acupuncture, floatation tanks, hypnosis, energy healing, and much more. Some of it has helped, some hasn't.

If you're at your wit's end, conventional medicine has failed you, and something, anything, gives a moment of light relief, grab it with both hands and say thanks for the temporary peace. Just don't go in expecting miracle cures, and be wary of any practitioner who says they can offer you one.

Look for guides

There are so many teachers out there.
People who have lived through their own
struggles and have abundant wisdom to share.
Listen to their podcasts, read their books,
try their meditations, join their mailing lists,
and let them light a path through the dark.

Some of the guides that have helped me in
my darkest moments include Pema Chödrön,
Tara Brach, Brené Brown, and Russ Harris.
Look for the guide that best suits your journey.

Be vulnerable

Ignore anyone who tells you that emotional resilience means you have to 'tough it out' or 'suck it up'. If you're struggling, be brave enough to be honest about it. You'd be surprised how warmly people respond when you show the soft underbelly we too often keep hidden.

Everyone knows what it's like to feel pain. Vulnerability is not a weakness, it's a strength. It's what connects us as humans.

Remember ...

Have faith in the goodness of people.
They will want to help.
Have the courage to let them.

6

Switch Off

I have a complicated relationship with my phone. It brings many benefits — FaceTiming with family on the other side of the world, getting lost in the murky corners of a true-crime podcast, keeping track of my steps as I smash my fitness goals, or scrolling through Instagram memories of past adventures and happy times spent with loved ones.

But then there are the times when it feels like I'm suffering from Stockholm Syndrome. Those days when I'm hopelessly enraptured with a captor who is destroying my life and will not let me go.

Being away from my phone makes me antsy. And yet the compulsive checking when it's within my reach makes me even more anxious. I know things are out of balance when I find myself unable to stop looking and my brain starts to feel like an overheated laptop, struggling to run dozens of open windows at once.

When I start exchanging furious tweets with people I disagree with or craving the validation of Instagram likes, it's usually a red flag for my mental health. I have to remind myself to stop, take a deep breath, and back away from my phone.

It remains a challenge to manage this love–hate relationship, but through the hardest times, I've learned some valuable lessons in how to take back control.

These are some tips not only on how to cut down the time you spend plugged into your phone, but on how to switch off from the world's woes long enough to regain some balance.

Turn off notifications

Is your phone lighting up like a Christmas tree, with flashing alerts and the constant ding-ding of notifications? Digital overload can make the brain feel heavy and overwhelmed. And for what purpose? You really don't need to be notified the minute some distant acquaintance comments 'cool sunset, dude' on your latest Instagram post. Turn them off.

Leave it at home

Your phone is not an extension of your body. It doesn't have to come with you every time you leave the house to buy a carton of milk or walk the dog. Leave it at home sometimes. It will be OK.

Clean up your home screen

How many apps on your phone do you actually need? Like, really need? If you find yourself mindlessly checking Facebook, Twitter, LinkedIn, Pinterest, or Snapchat every time there's a five-second pause at the pedestrian lights, perhaps it's time to delete them. I now only have Instagram on my phone, which has greatly reduced the amount of time I spend on other social platforms.

Pick your battles

Fighting with muppets on the internet
is bad for the soul. Before you fire off that
angry Facebook comment or get embroiled
in a Twitter war, ask yourself two
questions: 'What will this achieve?'
and 'Is it good for me?'

It's not your responsibility to challenge
every dumb or mean thing said on social
media. If you have to think twice about
whether what you're about to post is a good
idea, it probably isn't. Stay away from social
media and emails if you're tired, stressed,
drunk, or gripped by a white-hot rage.
If you must write it down, save it as a draft
and come back to it tomorrow.

Digital detox

When we're depleted, it's easy to fall into
a cycle of compulsive checking and scrolling
on our phones. Regular breaks from social
media, email, and other digital interactions will
introduce some calm. Screen-free weekends are
a good place to start, where you limit your
use of phones or tablets to calls only.

If you don't trust yourself not to pick up
your phone or open your laptop, you could
follow the lead of author Nikki Gemmell,
who describes in her fabulous book *On Quiet*
how she quietened her family time by buying
a small safe to lock away all their devices
at weekends!

Lock yourself out

The hypnotic lure of the internet can be
hard to resist with willpower alone. If you
have work to do, or just want to read a book
or watch a movie without the temptation of
reaching for your phone, download an app that
locks you out of social media, specific apps,
or the entire internet for a set period of time.
I use one called Freedom, but there is a whole
range to choose from, and many of
them are free.

Turn off the news

It's OK to turn away from bad news when you're not feeling great. Consuming too much negative news can make us view the world as more threatening than it is, adding to our angst.

Limiting exposure to the worst horrors of the daily news cycle is not burying your head in the sand, it's an exercise in self-replenishment. You can't change the world if you're too overwhelmed to act. Give yourself permission to switch off now and then.

Dr Google
is not
a real doctor

If, like me, you're prone to intermittent
fits of hypochondria and have diagnosed
yourself with everything from anthrax to zinc
poisoning, it's best not to trawl the internet
for evidence of your imminent death.

That rash on your arm is most likely not
evidence that you're about to succumb to
a fatal meningococcal disease. But if you're
really worried, choose a visit to a real-world
medical professional over an anxiety-peaking
afternoon spent wading through the weeds
of Reddit's 'Ask A Doctor'.

Bury your head in a book

When you're finding it difficult to
stop looking at your phone, books are
a great way to get out of your own head
and into someone else's head entirely.
What does escapism look like to you?
Is it reading a potboiler crime novel?
Or losing yourself in the Harry Potter
series? Pick a read that transports you
away from the chatter and into
a completely different world.

And if your brain is too busy to
concentrate on words on the page,

try listening to podcasts or audiobooks.
There's something soothing and
absorbing about listening to someone
tell you a story.

Breaking free

Phone addiction is real. We are pleasure-seeking animals and our brains have become habituated to craving the dopamine hit that comes from looking at that screen. If you're finding it hard to limit time on your devices, know that you're not alone. But you can wean your brain off its blue-light dependency.

Turn your phone to silent or flight mode and set an alarm to go off every 15 minutes. When it sounds, you have exactly one minute to check whatever you want to check on your phone. When the minute is up, turn the phone off again and repeat the process.

Once you've got used to 15-minute periods
you can step it up to 20, then 25, then 30,
and so on. It takes practice, but it works.
Your mind will slow down and stop
craving that hit.

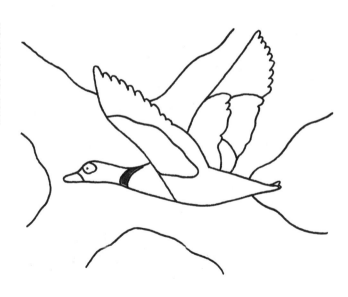

Remember ...

Sometimes you need to unplug
before you can recharge.

7

Clear Your Head

My brain races. A lot. I can't remember a time when my head wasn't filled with a rapid-fire stream of thoughts being yelled at me in the style of an over-stimulated sports commentator calling the final moments of a particularly nail-biting football match. Anxiety is fun like that.

When things get really bad, the chatter can be overwhelming. All that noise is hard to tune out. But there are ways to turn down the volume. It's a skill I'm still mastering, but I'm getting better at managing my many, many, many, many thoughts.

Here are a few tricks I've learned that can act as a circuit-breaker and help bring calm and order to an overly active mind that feels impossibly full with worry and stress.

Lists are our friend

If your 'to do' list is so overwhelming you feel paralysed, break it down into bite-sized chunks.

Write down everything you need to do — from the very basic (have a shower) to the more challenging (prepare tax return) — and number each item in order of urgency. What has to be done immediately? What can wait a bit longer?

Don't give an item any headspace until its number comes up. Only move on to number two once you've ticked off number one. And so on.

Journal
your thoughts

Keep a journal. Get your thoughts out
of your head and onto the page — every
irrational fear, every twisted emotion and
doomsday scenario. Don't edit yourself. Let
your thoughts flow from mind to pen in a
stream-of-consciousness brain dump.

I honestly don't know where I'd be if
I didn't regularly journal. It's like opening
a pressure valve. It doesn't have to make
sense, and you don't need to read it back. But
getting words on the page is therapeutic.

So much of our emotional distress is
driven by unconscious factors that are

often opaque to us. Journalling can help bring those hidden fears and dysfunctional patterns to consciousness. I'm continually amazed by what pops up when I put pen to the page. Knowing what lies underneath the anxiety makes it easier to manage.

Note to self

'I can't handle this' — a common and
recurring thought on the tough days.
You can. You have. And you will. But
it can be hard to remember that when
you're in the eye of the storm.

After the storm has passed, take a
moment to write a note to yourself about
how you survived and how you can again.
Give credit to your strength, and list the
lies your brain tells you, noting that despite
the trickery, you got through. Refer to
the note next time you feel like you
can't make it.

Declutter

You don't have to go full Marie Kondo and cull your entire wardrobe or tidy every last elastic band and safety pin into neat little boxes (although I have done this, and it was surprisingly cathartic). But a quick declutter can be cleansing. Creating physical space can also help clear space in your mind.

Start small — a drawer or a cupboard — and throw out anything in it you don't need or haven't used for more than a year. Commit to tidying this one area. But if you finish and find you want to keep going, have a crack at another drawer or cupboard, or even a whole room.

Compile a
watch list

On those days when the news gets too
depressing, your thoughts are crowding in
on you, and the world seems to be teetering
on the brink of the apocalypse, switch off
and go watch your favourite fun TV show.
Make a list of movies or shows you can rely
on to help you cheer up or tune out on
the difficult days.

Ru Paul's Drag Race is my favourite gateway
to escapism because who wouldn't be cheered
up by a troupe of sassy drag queens sashaying
down the runway and having wig-raising cat
fights as they 'lip synch for their life' in
six-inch heels? The life advice alone is worth

the price of admission. As Ru says at the end of each episode, 'If you can't love yourself, how in the hell you gonna love somebody else?' Amen, sister.

Does it matter?

If that thing you're freaking out
about won't matter this time next week,
next month, or next year, it probably
doesn't matter.

Change your perspective

Literally. Lie on the floor. Choose a different spot on the couch. Find a corner of your home you rarely occupy and spend some time there.

When you're stressing out over a difficult life event or obsessing about that intractable thing that seems to have no solution, looking at the world from a different position can help unscramble your thoughts.

What if?

An anxious brain will try to set up camp in the future. It wants to live in a world of 'what ifs', where everything that could go wrong, will go wrong. *What if this is a failure? What if she never speaks to me again? What if I have a rare and incurable cancer and all my hair falls out?*

These are just thoughts. View them as flotsam and jetsam in a fast-flowing river. Stay on the bank and watch them float past. Don't jump in and get swept up in the current. The thoughts only have power if you attach significance to them.

Read the signs

After more emotional meltdowns than I can count, I've become intimately familiar with the red flags that let me know things are starting to unravel. These include trying to reason with ideologues on Twitter, becoming overly needy with my friends, and using wine as an anaesthetic.

Get to know your own warning signs. Write them down in a place that's easy to access, and refer to them regularly to keep yourself in check. Being aware of the signs helps you get back on track before things spiral.

Fifty shades of grey

When we're in struggle town, it can be easy to fall into black-or-white thinking. 'If I lose this job, my career is over.' 'I always screw things up.' 'We had that fight again, and they'll never forgive me.'

But nothing is ever as good or as bad as it seems. The truth is usually found in the many shades of grey in between. Try to limit your use of words like 'never' and 'always', and challenge whether this absolute thinking is accurate. Look for evidence to counter the black and white.

Remember ...

Thoughts are not facts.

8

Live in the Small

When you're not OK, problems can seem impossibly big. Whether it's the woes of the world when you turn on the news or the stresses in your own life, the negatives become amplified to full volume and the positives get drowned out by the noise.

At times like these, it can be helpful to narrow your lens from the big picture to a more tightly focused perspective. Honing in on the simple stuff can bring joy and calm. These are some tips on how to find comfort from living in the small.

Gratitude works

Each night before bed I write down three
things that went well that day or that
I'm grateful for. Gratitude doesn't mean
plastering a smile on your face and pretending
everything's fine while your house burns down
around you. It's a reminder that even on the
darkest days there's always a chink of light.

Regularly practising gratitude has been shown
to change the way our brains process events.
It can lower stress and activate dopamine, the
'feel-good' chemical. Over time, your mind
starts to actively seek out positives you might
otherwise have missed, making it easier
to cope with the tough stuff.

Jar of joy

If you prefer your gratitude to come in a more visual form, try this. Buy some coloured paper and cut it up into small squares. When something happens that makes you pause to give thanks, or someone does something nice for you, write it down on a square, fold it up, and put it in a jar.

At the end of the year, pick a day to open every square and enjoy your jar full of reasons to be grateful.

Small wins

It's hard to see the good stuff when an over-active mind drags you to the bleakest outlook. When I was really struggling, I used a wall-calendar sticker system to remind me of my wins.

Green was for exercise, blue for meditation, yellow was for when I got out of bed before 9.00 am, red was for eating, and pink was for when I was kind to myself and didn't act on the irrational thoughts my brain conjured up. I even had a smiley face for those wonderful days when life seemed manageable again.

The stickers helped me note correlations between my mood and my actions, proving I was not helpless. And when my inner critic told me I had achieved nothing or was going backwards, the riot of colour on my calendar offered a different story.

These days, I use an app called My Year In Pixels, which lets me assign each day one of five colours, from red (the absolute worst) to green (amazing). In tough times, when my brain tells me 'you've always been miserable', the colour chart shows me the much more positive truth of the previous weeks and months.

Listen to the rain on the roof

Turn the TV off. Unplug your music.
Put down your phone. Shut your eyes.
Just listen.

Bookmark joy

The internet can be a dark place, but it can also provide a quick burst of joy when you need it most. Bookmark a YouTube clip that makes you laugh or lifts you up. For me, it's a video of a group of baby pandas sliding down a slide at a nature sanctuary. Look it up — two minutes of unadulterated joy.

The money trap

Retail therapy has its place — ugg boots and a set of comfy pyjamas are a solid investment in yourself when you need nurturing — but you don't need to spend big to gain comfort.

The advertising industry wants you to believe the lie that you are not enough — not thin enough, rich enough, attractive enough, relaxed enough. But if you just lose five kilos, buy this luxury car, sign up to this boot camp, or order these breathable yoga pants, you could be.

Don't fall for it. The research consistently shows money doesn't buy happiness. The more stuff we have, the more we crave. The greater the choice, the deeper the paralysis. Pare it right back. When it comes to contentment, less is definitely more.

Sing

At the top of your voice. Belt out your favourite songs and don't hold back. Really give it everything. Feel the music deep in your lungs and your bones.

Have hope

It's often when we're in a place of hopelessness that the power of hope reveals itself. As Auschwitz survivor Viktor Frankl observed in his memoir *Man's Search for Meaning*, 'Everything can be taken from a man but one thing: the last of the human freedoms — to choose one's attitude in any given set of circumstances, to choose one's own way.'

You always have choices. Even if it's just going back to basics and choosing to keep breathing in and out and putting one foot in front of the other until it's no longer an effort. Hope is always there.

Good news

Bad news makes headlines. Good news not so much. This constant stream of negativity can skew our view of the world and lead to a sense of learned helplessness. Biologically, we're hardwired to react to bad news because when we sense danger it triggers the body's fight-or-flight response, prompting us to pay attention.

So if we want to see the reasons to be hopeful — and there are many — we have to actively seek them out. Dive into websites like Positive News or Good News Network, which, instead of focusing on what's going wrong, provide a unique perspective on all the things that are going right in the world.

Look for the helpers

The world can be cruel and brutal at times, but whenever there is tragedy or adversity the number of people showing courage, compassion, and kindness always vastly outweighs the small minority who would turn away or do us harm.

Children's TV host Fred Rogers famously said that when he saw scary things on the news his mum told him, 'Look for the helpers. You will always find people who are helping.'

Look for the people running towards the burning building and the ones who offer comfort to strangers. Look for those little moments of kindness and connection that remind us of our shared humanity.

Be happy
in between

Life's purest joys are not found in the
happy-ever-after, but in the happy-in-between:
those moments of connection with a loved
one; a sky so perfectly blue it looks painted on;
the blissful abandon of a dog running full
tilt off-leash in the park.

Try not to focus on a grand end goal or
prize — the job, the partner, the home,
the weight loss. Instead, pay attention to
the little things. Enjoy the moment, but don't
try to hold it captive or chase an encore.
Appreciate it for what it is: an exquisite
snapshot in time.

Remember ...

It's possible to struggle
and still be strong.

9

You Do You

I've wasted far too many hours of my life wishing I was someone else. I've agonised over my flaws, obsessed about my weirdness, and compared myself to friends, celebrities, colleagues, and strangers on the internet — all while imagining how much happier/richer/thinner/cooler/more popular I'd be if only I could be like them.

I try not to do that anymore. It's not that I no longer care what people think — because, let's be honest, if not giving a fuck was actually a subtle art form, rather than a life-long tussle with our own brains, we'd all be high-kicking our way through the world like Beyoncé at the Super Bowl — it's just that I've come to care more about what *I* think.

One of the greatest lessons I've learned over the past few years is that if I want to minimise my chances of falling headfirst into a rabbit hole of anxiety and depression, I have to muster the courage to not just passively follow the pack, but consciously choose a path that nurtures and sustains me. That means learning to stop comparing myself to everyone else and to start celebrating me in all of my glorious weirdness. It means pursuing what actually brings me joy, fulfilment, and calm and making no apologies for it.

We spend so much of our lives weighed down by expectation, duty, and guilt. We follow the herd or pursue paths we didn't choose to please others who are living their dreams vicariously through us. It can make it difficult to remember what it is that really makes our hearts sing.

But when we have the courage to back ourselves, drop the comparisons, and start becoming our own cheerleaders, life becomes much more fulfilling and easier to navigate.

Hey jealousy

When things are tough, seeing shiny-faced wellness influencers, with their flawless lives, declare that 'happiness is a choice' makes me want to either weep or put my fist through the wall. I have to remind myself that if I'm going to be jealous of someone's life, I have to be jealous of all of it — not just the social-media highlights reel.

Despite what Instagram's fairytale filter would have us believe, nobody's life is perfect. Try not to compare yourself to people who boast about being #blessed and #livingmybestlife and instead see it for what it is — a carefully curated piece of public theatre.

If it's too hard to believe that everyone on your social-media feed hasn't got their shit together and is, like all of us, doubting themselves daily, then consider taking a break from looking until you feel stronger.

Don't chase haters

Despite what you might have learned at high school, you don't have to take part in the popularity contest. Not everyone is going to like you, and that's OK.

Chasing the approval of people who don't deserve your attention is wasted energy. Let the haters hate, and know that it says more about them than it does about you. As one of my favourite drag queens from *Ru Paul's Drag Race*, Sharon Needles, astutely points out, 'Boos are just applause from ghosts.'

Embrace
JOMO

Don't be a slave to FOMO (fear of missing out).
Open your arms to JOMO (the joy of missing
out). The absolute thrill of knowing you're
doing exactly what you *want* to do, not what
you feel you *should* do.

Be brave, and run your own race. If you'd rather
snuggle under a blanket on the couch with
your dog and a tub of mint choc chip gelato
than go to that banging house party, then stay
home and celebrate your decisions.

My greatest expression of JOMO is my annual
New Year's Eve ritual, where I forgo the
collective celebrations and have my very own

party for one at home. Candles, a good movie,
a block of chocolate, freshly laundered pyjamas,
and tunes that uplift my soul — bliss. Find your
ritual, and revel in your choices.

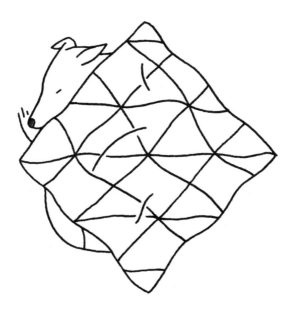

Get 'should' in the bin

When 'should' becomes our driving force, we risk being crushed under its weight. I should be thinner. I should be happy. I should stay in this job. I should be enjoying this party. I should be married by now.

Nope. The only thing you should be doing is letting go of the pressure to live your life according to other people's expectations and start figuring out what truly brings you joy, fulfilment, and calm. Then do that.

You complete you

I'm sure I'm not the first person to say these words, but Tom Cruise was wrong. 'You complete me' is a crock. Don't believe you're somehow broken without a partner to make you complete. Wholeness is not something we can sub-contract to another. It's an entirely internal affair.

Trying to get your validation and self-worth from external sources is like pouring water into a leaky bucket. There will never be enough to fill you up. If you feel incomplete, then know that *you* are the missing puzzle piece.

Instead of fearing solitude, recognise that it's normal and healthy. Spending time alone has been shown to foster creativity, boost self-knowledge and compassion, and even lower stress. Carve out time for yourself, and embrace going solo.

A table for one

Get out your calendar, and lock in dates
with yourself. Be brave enough to go to a movie
or have dinner on your own. Indulge yourself
with a picnic in the park, an ice-cream sundae
the size of your head, a long soak in a bath,
or whatever brings you joy.

Treat these dates as if they were a commitment
to a dear friend. Don't cancel or postpone.
This is your time to slow down and reconnect
with yourself.

You Do You

127

Banish guilt

It's not selfish to schedule in a whole afternoon to do nothing but read a book or watch your favourite TV show. It's an act of self-replenishment. Downtime often restores you to tackle the stuff you find hard to face.

Ditch the pain olympics

Your pain is valid. No matter how big
or small the problem, it's real. Comparing
your emotional suffering to someone else's
is a pointless exercise. It's not a competition.
There will always be someone worse or better
off than you. Instead of trying to deny your
problems are legitimate, give yourself
credit for acknowledging they exist.

Know your
limits

'You can't hold up a friend when your
own arm is broken.' This is something my
psychologist often says to me as a reminder
to know my own limits. If you're depleted
or not in a good place, it's hard to support
someone else who's struggling.

It's OK to step back and take care of yourself.
Think of it like the oxygen masks on an
aeroplane. You have to make sure your own
mask is secure first, before you can assist those
around you. Practise setting boundaries
and putting yourself first.

Self-care has no price tag

Doing the right thing by yourself is important. But self-care needn't break the bank. Sure, if you can afford to pamper yourself with a weekend break, a full-body massage, or an afternoon at a day spa, then go for it.

But booking into a luxury hinterland resort with an infinity pool overlooking the ocean is far less important than simply showing yourself some love, right here in this moment.

Remember ...

The only approval you need
is your own.

Be Kind to Yourself
(and Others)

Think about the way you talk to yourself. Would you talk to a friend in the same way? When you're feeling bruised and vulnerable, being mean and hyper-critical about your perceived mistakes and failures is a common trap. But it only makes things worse.

Believe me, I have a long history of beating myself up in cruel and inventive ways, so I know what it's like to battle a voice that constantly tries to undermine, bully, and berate. Offering loving-kindness to the part of you that feels broken takes practice, but it's well worth the effort. When we're more forgiving, we can move through our suffering more easily.

In a divided world where everyone seems to be retreating to their corner and angrily defending their position, it can be tough to offer that same loving-kindness to those around us, but letting go of anger has also been shown to have positive effects on our mental health. These are some things I've learned about how to live in a more kind and compassionate way.

The inner
critic

We all have one. Mine is a cross between
Nurse Ratched from *One Flew over the Cuckoo's
Nest* and Regina George from *Mean Girls*.
She used to control me with her relentless
reminders that I was a hopelessly broken loser
destined to die alone in a hovel reeking
of cat wee.

But now I see her as a character in a movie.
She's dramatic and cutting, and sometimes
even amusing, but as impressive as her
performance is, her critiques are just pre-
rehearsed lines that hold no basis in reality.
Get to know your inner critic and the
stories they tell you.

Respond to that voice in your head telling you you're not enough with compassion, not anger. It comes from a place of fear. Reassure, don't chastise. Treat yourself as you would a wounded child. Be loving, gentle, and forgiving. Practise kindness and patience. You are worth the effort.

Compassion heals

The Dalai Lama says, 'If you want others to be happy, practise compassion. If you want to be happy, practise compassion.' Science backs him up. Being compassionate stimulates the same pleasure centres associated with the drive for food, water, and sex. We are hard-wired to be kind.

It can increase calm, lower blood pressure, and boost immune response. When we recognise common fears and vulnerabilities rather than focus on differences, it calms the nervous system and increases feelings of contentment and self-worth. Offer kindness to those around you, and watch how much lighter you feel.

Think the best of people

Even when they're being dicks. You don't
know what else is going on in their lives.
Hurt people often hurt people. Everyone
is fighting a battle you can't see.

Do something nice

There's a reason some billionaires donate large swathes of their fortune to charity — giving feels good. Random acts of kindness — whether extended to a loved one or a complete stranger — can produce a temporary burst of happiness, particularly if you're struggling with your own anxieties.

Whether it's volunteering with a charity or just sending a card to tell someone you appreciate them, shifting the focus from the internal to the external can be a circuit-breaker for an overly active brain.

Anger burns

How often do you feel better when you scream at the driver who cut you off in traffic or belittle the call-centre operator who can't answer your questions? That temporary release of pressure usually comes back to bite you.

Anger is corrosive. When you pick up a hot coal to throw at someone, you only end up with burnt hands. Before responding to a situation or person you feel has wronged you, take five deep breaths and pause. Imagine how you'll feel if you lash out. Could you try a different way?

Try a little tenderness

After living with anxiety and panic attacks
for many years, I've become quite skilled at
self-soothing. I'm gentler in the way I talk to
myself, but I also find touch can be calming.

If you're freaking out, try placing a hand
on your heart or stroking the back of your
hand. If it helps, calm the part of you that's
panicking by offering words of reassurance.
I sometimes say, 'It's OK, darling, I've got you,'
or, 'I'm here, you are loved.' Show yourself
some physical tenderness the way you would
care for a loved one.

Music to feed
the soul

Make a playlist of your favourite uplifting
songs to help survive the days that seem
impossible and remind you of your
awesomeness. Mine is called *You Are Amazing,*
and it's jam-packed with tunes that feel
like a hug or a high-five.

My absolute blue-day anthem is Andra
Day's 'Rise Up'. A reminder that I've been
down on the canvas before, and I got back up.
And I'll do it a thousand times again.
Find your anthem. Play it loud.

Play like you're a kid

When we're kids, we play simply because it's fun. Then we grow up and get crushed under the weight of adult responsibility and self-consciousness, and we come to view playtime as selfish, foolish, and indulgent. But that playful nature still burns inside us. And there's no greater act of self-care than when we tap into it.

Let yourself be playful again. Write a list of stuff that is fun, relaxing, or joyful for its own sake. Refer to the list whenever you need to reconnect to yourself. It could be baking the favourite cookies you had growing up, pottering in the garden,

or rocking out the air guitar in
your kitchen.

My list includes belting out songs from
Frozen in my underwear in the kitchen,
eating takeaway pizza on the couch while
binge watching a serial-killer show, and
throwing a silent disco for one in the park,
where I dance with my headphones on like
no one's watching — even if someone is.

Ditch perfect

Don't let perfect be the enemy of good.
It's so easy to feel that you might as well
throw in the towel if you haven't managed to
stick precisely to your carefully laid-out plans
or reach every single one of your goals.

But if you end up going for a walk instead
of a five-kilometre run, you're still lapping
everyone who's at home on the couch. Give
yourself a break. It's OK not to be perfect.
Perfect is boring.

One step forward ...

Progress is a measure of increments over a lifetime, not an overnight transformation or a state of Zen-like utopia where you never make a mistake. Life isn't as simple as 'success' or 'failure'. It's often one step forward, a few steps back, and a whole lot of steps sideways.

Accept that you're going to stumble and that at times it will feel like you're going backwards. But look at change as a long game. Measure yourself not against where you were this time last week, but where you were this time last year or five or ten years ago. Celebrate the wins. Every single one of them.

Remember ...

You are enough.
Just as you are.

Acknowledgements

To Henry, Anna, Cora, Al, and the whole team at Scribe — heartfelt thanks for your continued enthusiasm for my ideas and for the care you take in helping me craft them into something I'm proud to share with the world. And a huge thank you to Carla McRae for the exquisite illustrations.

To my friends and family, thank you for lifting me up. I'm so lucky to be loved and supported by this wonderful village of helpers. And a special shout-out to Jason and Nonie for your compassion, care, and endless patience when anxiety has me in its teeth. When I'm not ok, you help me find my strength.

And to my incredible readers, who have shared with me their own stories of navigating tough times — your courage and willingness to trust me with your vulnerability is the reason I write.